MY ART IS SO LOUD
POEMS AND PLAYS FROM

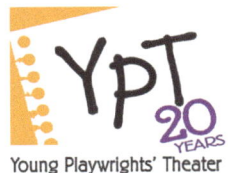

Special thanks to the following individuals for their support in bringing **The 524 Project** to Western International High School (Detroit) and Ballou Senior High School (Washington, DC) students. *My Art is So Loud* is a publication of the 2014 InsideOut Literary Arts Project (Detroit) and Young Playwrights' Theater (Washington, DC).

The 524 Project was supported by **The MetLife / TCG A-ha! Program** with additional support from the **Skillman Foundation** and the **National Endowment for the Arts**.

Detroit Public Schools Board of Education:
LaMar Lemmons (Pres.), Herman Davis (Vice Pres.), Jonathan Kinloch, Rev. David Murray, Ida Short, Tawanna Simpson, Elena M. Herrada, Annie Carter, Judy Summers, Wanda Redmond, and Juvette Hawkins-Williams

Western International High School
1500 Scotten Street
Detroit, MI 48209
www.detroit.k12.mi.us

Principal: Rodolfo Diaz
Faculty Advisor, Patrick Butler

The 524 Project *Writers-in-Residence:*
Mahogany Jones, Shawntai Brown,
Isaac Miller and Deirdre Skiles

InsideOut Executive Director & Founder:
Terry M. Blackhawk, Ph.D.;
Board of Directors: Rhonda Buckley, Maureen Clinesmith, Victor Green, Helen Dove-Jones, Denise Page Hood, Michelle Krebs, Dwight Levens, Mary Madigan, Bunice Robinson, April Royster, Phil Schloop, Linda Spight

For more information contact:
InsideOut Literary Arts Project
5143 Cass Ave., Room #225
WSU - State Hall Bldg.
Detroit, MI 48202
(313) 577-4601
www.insideoutdetroit.org

DC State Board of Education:
Mark Jones (Pres.), Mary Lord (Vice Pres.), D. Kamili Anderson, Jack Jacobson, Karen Williams, Laura McGiffert Slover, Monica Warren-Jones, Patrick Mara, Tierra Jolly

Ballou Senior High School
3401 4th Street SE
Washington, DC 20032
www.dcps.dc.gov

Principal: Rahman Branch
Faculty Advisors: Audra Polk & Darrell Watson

The 524 Project *Resident Teaching Artist:*
Gedalya Chinn
Assistant Teaching Artists:
Quilla Otto-Jacobs, Natalie Piegari

Young Playwrights' Theater Executive Director:
Brigitte Pribnow Moore.;
Founding Artistic Director: Karen Zacarías;
Board of Directors: Ben-James Brown, Jonathan Chace, Catherine Crum, Alicia Dick, Eric Fraint, Miriam Gonzales, Bryan Greene, Glenn S. Greene, Francine Hope, Karen Kok, Amy Kurz, Catherine Nagel, Julie Paller

For more information contact:
Young Playwrights' Theater
2437 15th St. NW
Washington, DC 20009
(202) 387-9173
www.youngplaywrightstheater.org

THE 524 PROJECT STUDENTS

DETROIT:

Adrian Casillas
Ashley Gonzalez
Brayan Sanchez
Carrie Roper
Daleecea McDaniel
Diego Vasquez
Dorian Bryant
Elijah Wakefield
Esmerelda Barco
Felix Lee
Hector Montigo
Jackie Llamas
Jessica Arias
Jessica Chavero
José Lopez
José Hernandez
Josua Salazar
Katrina Ramirez
Keishla Rios
Kimmy Nguyen
Leo Culver
Melida Villarreal
Moises Diaz
Morgan Michael
Olivia Thumsey
Orlando Stevens
Rosario Ramirez
Terrell Jackson
Tony Saucedo
Vanessa Sanchez

DC:

Akim DeVille
Antonio Anderson
Brittany Spencer
Callie Bizzell
Damarco Morgan
Da'Nae Giles
Destini Simmons
Dwayne Whittaker
Emoni Lowery
Iesha Crawford
Isaiah Prophet
Kyra Sheppard
Lamara Brooks
Nadiya Holley
Precious Starks
Shawn Lee
Shawnquinette Davis
Sharhonda Lewis
Tanisha Phillips
Tiana Minter-El
Will Richardson

TABLE OF CONTENTS

9   Introduction

12   **The 524 Project** Word Clouds (DC pre-program)
14   **The 524 Project** Word Clouds (DC post-program)

DC VIGNETTE 1: I AM

16   I Am DC, *Brittany Spencer*
          I Am DC, *Damarco Morgan*
17   I Am DC, *Shawn Lee*

18   **The 524 Project** Word Clouds (Detroit pre-program)
20   **The 524 Project** Word Clouds (Detroit post-program)

DETROIT VIGNETTE 1: I AM

22   I Am Detroit, *Leo Culver*
23   I Am Detroit, *Adrian Casillas*
          I Am Detroit, *Diego Vasquez*

DC VIGNETTE 2: PERSPECTIVES IN CONFLICT

24   DC, Years from Now, *Will Richardson*
          I Am DC, *Shawnquinette Davis*
25   Taking the Tree Out of the Glitz of DC, *Da'Nae Giles*
26   DC and the Media, *Isaiah Prophet*

DETROIT VIGNETTE 2: MY ART IS SO LOUD

28   My Art is So Loud, *Josua Salazar*
29   My Art is So Loud, *Dorian Bryant*
          My Art is So Loud, *Felix Lee*
          My Art is So Loud, *Jessica Arias*

DC VIGNETTE 3: ...AND SO IS MINE (MY ART IS SO LOUD, PT. 2)

30   My Art is So Loud, *Callie Bizzell, Emoni Lowery, Sharhonda Lewis,
          Tanisha Phillips and Tiana Minter-El*
31   My Art is So Loud, *Brittany Spencer, Da'Nae Giles,
          Iesha Crawford, Nadiya Holley and Will Richardson*
          My Art is So Loud, *Akim DeVille, Antonio Anderson,
          Damarco Morgan, Isaiah Prophet and Shawn Lee*

DETROIT VIGNETTE 3: SCENES OF THE CITY
32   Welcome to Detroit, *José Lopez*
33   Society Against Outcast, *Rosario Ramirez*
34   Scenes of the City, *Anonymous*

DC VIGNETTE 4: LOVE AND OTHER WORDS
36   Love, *Sharhonda Lewis (Performed by Precious Starks)*
37   Love Letter to Detroit, *Callie Bizzell*
      Love Letter to Detroit, *Akim DeVille*
38   Love Letter to Detroit, *Emoni Lowery*
      Love Letter to Detroit, *Tanisha Phillips*
39   Love Letter to Detroit, *Destini Simmons*
40   Love Letter to Detroit, *Nadiya Holley*

DETROIT VIGNETTE 4: ROMANTIC POINT OF VIEW
42   Love Me, *Daleecea McDaniel*
43   Romance, *Jackie Llamas*
44   Romance, *Jessica Chavero*
      Romance, *Leo Culver*

DC VIGNETTE 5: FREE YOUR VOICE... AND THE REST WILL FOLLOW
46   What I See in My School, *Lamara Brooks*
47   Just a List of Things: Cars, Football and Them J's,
      Shawnquinette Davis
      I Am a Penny, *Iesha Crawford*
48   5 Years Ago, *Kyra Sheppard*
      Crack Pipe, *Lamara Brooks (Performed by Dwayne Whittaker)*
49   The Go-Go DC Spoken Word Piece, *Tiana Minter-El*

DETROIT VIGNETTE 5: MY VOICE
50   All I See, *Esmerelda Barco*
51   Life, *Olivia Thumsey*
      My Neighborhood, *Jose Hernandez*

53   **The 524 Project** Assessment Results
59   The Organizations

INTRODUCTION

DC and Detroit: two cities that loom large in the national imagination. Too frequently, these cities are presented to the world as centers of extreme poverty, high crime and violence, with little recognition of their rich cultural histories. Young people in both cities grow up struggling with these stereotypes, torn between the vibrant worlds they see around them and the desolation they see on TV.

They have stories to tell, but no opportunity to tell them. **The 524 Project** was created to give them that opportunity.

Early in 2013, a team of theater educators from DC-based Young Playwrights' Theater (YPT) travelled to Detroit and met the amazing poets who lead InsideOut Literary Arts Project (iO). As two organizations dedicated to empowering young people through creative writing, YPT and iO became fast friends and committed to finding a way to collaborate. Their mission: work with young people in both cities to bridge the 524 miles between Detroit and DC using playwriting, poetry and 21st century technology to complicate the narratives of both places and empower students to share their own stories.

Six months later, thanks to a MetLife/TCG A-ha! Do It grant, **The 524 Project** became a reality. Collaborating in-person and online, YPT and iO co-designed an arts curriculum that incorporated playwriting and poetry into a broader conversation about personal and civic identity. In February, 2014, they brought this pilot program to two classrooms – one at Ballou Senior High School in Washington, DC and one at Western International High School in Detroit.

Every Wednesday that semester, **The 524 Project** team taught the same lesson plan simultaneously to students at Ballou and Western. Using prompts such as "I Am [City Name]" and "City-to-City Love Letters," students created original poems, monologues and

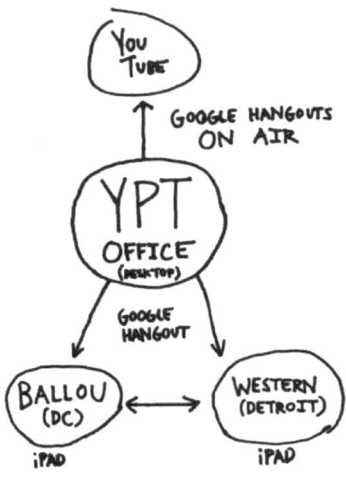

scenes inspired by conversations about their cities. Equipped with iPads retrofitted with digital video technology, YPT and iO then connected the two classes over Google Hangouts for live exchanges of student work and reflections on the dominant narratives of both cities. (Special thanks to our friends at Meridian Hill Pictures for providing the technical expertise needed to make these exchanges a reality!) We also broadcast our students' dramatic and poetic writing online via our Tumblr "blogumentary," empowering our young artists to reclaim their cities' legacies on a national scale. Through weekly digest videos, photos from the classroom and a host of other content, **The 524 Project** students discussed, created, owned and shared a new vision of their hometowns' pasts, presents and futures.

The 524 Project culminated in a student-generated, multimedia final presentation of poems, scenes and other pieces that presented an authentic, nuanced view of two cities damaged by stereotypes and misconceptions. Performed live in both DC and Detroit, and live-streamed on YouTube, the final presentation could be seen not just in both cities, but across the world! After taking their bows, our students held an impromptu dance-off over yet another live Google Hangout, capping the entire project with a joyful celebration of all they had accomplished together. As *Detroit Metro Times* journalist Larry Gabriel wrote in his review of the presentation: "These students have stepped up to assert that we are so much more than what you see of us on television and in the news."

The 524 Project was an incredible learning experience not only for our students, but for both organizations as well. The technical demands of the project were unlike anything YPT or iO has ever faced, and the process of empowering young people to see their cities through the eyes of another proved more complex than we first anticipated. But, in the end, the students took the lead, and told their stories more truthfully and powerfully than we could have dreamed. In the words of Western student Leo Culver's "I Am Detroit" poem: "I am the diamond in the rough — the up-and-coming underdog. / I am the small glare of light in the darkness."

What follows is a compilation of student work from both Detroit and DC, highlighting the many poignant, insightful and sometimes funny ways in which our students said, "I speak for my city." We have also included the results of our pre- and post- assessments, which demonstrate that the program had a significant impact in our students' lives. If you would like to learn more about **The 524 Project**, we encourage you to visit our tumblr page at www.524project.tumblr.com – there you will find all the triumphs, failures and faceplants of this exciting journey!

We'd love nothing more than for you to learn from our process, and then take our idea and make it your own. Imagine how much our young people could grow if students from San Francisco collaborated with students in Dallas, who passed their lives along to Chicago, who shared their world with St. Louis, New York, Paris and Cape Town. The opportunity exists—all it needs is a few dedicated champions. That's why we're here today. We hope you enjoy the journey, and that it inspires you to dream boldly.

Warmly,

Alise Alousi
Associate Director

Brigitte Pribnow Moore,
Executive Director

BALLOU SENIOR HIGH SCHOOL, WASHINGTON DC

PRE-PROGRAM

WHAT COMES TO MIND WHEN YOU THINK OF DC?

My Art Is So Loud

WHAT COMES TO MIND WHEN YOU THINK OF DETROIT?

EMINEM VIOLENCE FORD
TEMPTATIONS
FEMALES
CRIME
GUNS ACCENT SHUT DOWN COLD BUILDINGS
PISTONS MOTOWN
MUSIC
THUGS
BORING
TACK
BIG SEAN
RAPPERS
BAD ECONOMY
POVERTY GANGS CARS GHETTO
PHONE
BIG CITY
I DON'T KNOW NOTHING
BANKRUPT LIONS 8 MILE
GM D-12
DRUGS
CLUBS
GRAFFITI AUTO FACTORIES
KS. POLK DREADS
TRUCKS
NO WORDS COME TO MIND
CONNECTED TO CANADA
VACANT HOUSES HOUSE MUSIC
MURDER CAPITAL
KROGER MARIJUANA CHRYSLER
FAKE HAIR
SLANG DEATH
GUN VIOLENCE LOUD MUSIC
A LOT OF SHOOTING KIDS THROUGH THE AGES OF 14-18
AUTO
MOTOR CITY
801
MICHIGAN
DETROIT RIVER
HAIR
BANDO
FOOD
N/A
URBAN DECAY
UNEMPLOYED
7 MILE
KID ROCK
TWERKING

KEY

People and Demographics

Positive Traits

Negative Traits

Learned/Discussed in 524 Project

Local Sports, Pop Culture and Fashion

Poverty, Crime and Social Issues

Local Industry (Auto or Government)

Geography and Landmarks

*Poems and Plays from **The 524 Project***   13

BALLOU SENIOR HIGH SCHOOL, WASHINGTON DC

POST-PROGRAM

WHAT COMES TO MIND WHEN YOU THINK OF DC?

My Art Is So Loud

WHAT COMES TO MIND WHEN YOU THINK OF DETROIT?

MOTOWN EMINEM FORD
THE 524 PROJECT URBAN DECAY
DEBT MS. POLK POVERTY IN DEBT
BLACK ON BLACK CRIME
I DON'T REMEMBER TIGER
D-12 TALENTED 85% BLACK
MOTOR CITY VIOLENCE LIONS
GRAFFITI
BANKRUPT MICHIGAN CARS
THEY DRESS WELL
BOTTLED WATER
VACANT HOUSING
A GREAT CITY
WESTERN INTERNATIONAL HS GHETTO
I DON'T THINK ABOUT DETROIT GANGS
BANKRUPTCY A BAND CALLED DEATH BANDOS GUNS
DIVERSITY OPEN-MINDED
RESPECTFUL
FRESH WATER
HIGH CRIME RATES
MURDER CAPITAL

KEY

- Local Sports, Pop Culture and Fashion
- Poverty, Crime and Social Issues
- Local Industry (Auto or Government)
- Geography and Landmarks
- People and Demographics
- Positive Traits
- Negative Traits
- Learned/Discussed in 524 Project

DC VIGNETTE 1:
I AM

I AM DC
by *Brittany Spencer*

I am DC.
You think you know me.
You think I'm full of violence.
But really...
...I am historical and legendary.

I AM DC
by *Damarco Morgan*

I am DC, to the fullest.
You think you know me as a drug-filled wasteland that doesn't
   care about life,
but really I am well-educated,
street smart,
and I have the potential to become as successful as I want to be.

I AM DC

by *Shawn Lee*

I am DC.

You think you know me.

You think I'm a place of depression, hatred,
  and also a place of poor education.

Actually, I am a place where dreams and nightmares are made.
A place where lives are made and taken. Where people aspire to
get money and will do whatever to obtain it. A place that isn't just
expensive clothes and slang words, but a place where laws are made
and legends are born.

WESTERN INTERNATIONAL HIGH SCHOOL, DETROIT

PRE-PROGRAM

WHAT COMES TO MIND WHEN YOU THINK OF DETROIT?

WHAT COMES TO MIND WHEN YOU THINK OF DC?

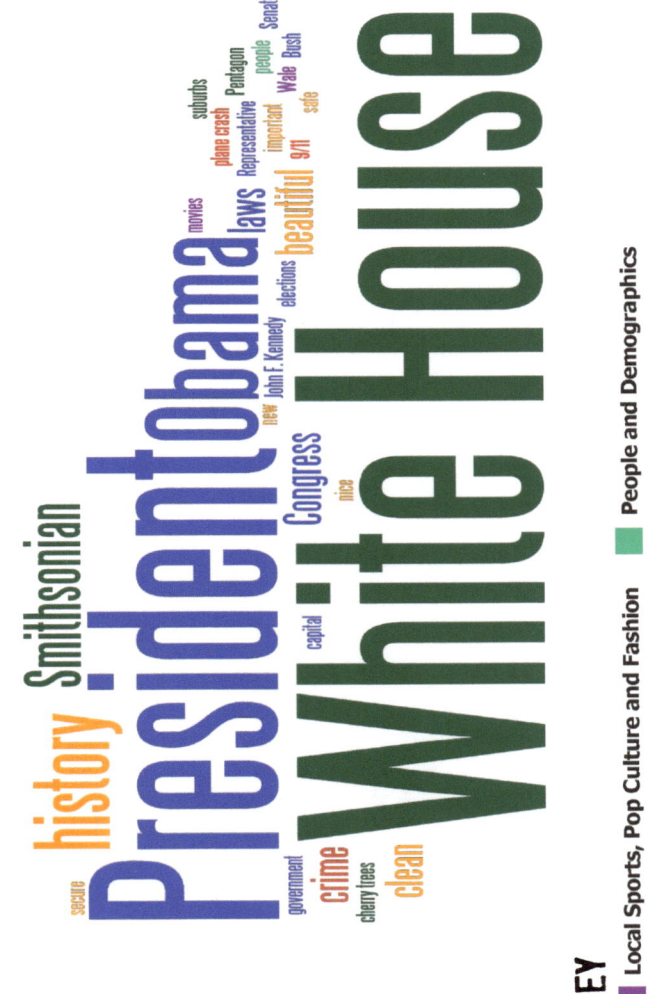

KEY

- Local Sports, Pop Culture and Fashion
- Poverty, Crime and Social Issues
- Local Industry (Auto or Government)
- Geography and Landmarks
- People and Demographics
- Positive Traits
- Negative Traits
- Learned/Discussed in 524 Project

WESTERN INTERNATIONAL HIGH SCHOOL, DETROIT

POST-PROGRAM

WHAT COMES TO MIND WHEN YOU THINK OF DETROIT?

My Art Is So Loud

WHAT COMES TO MIND WHEN YOU THINK OF DC?

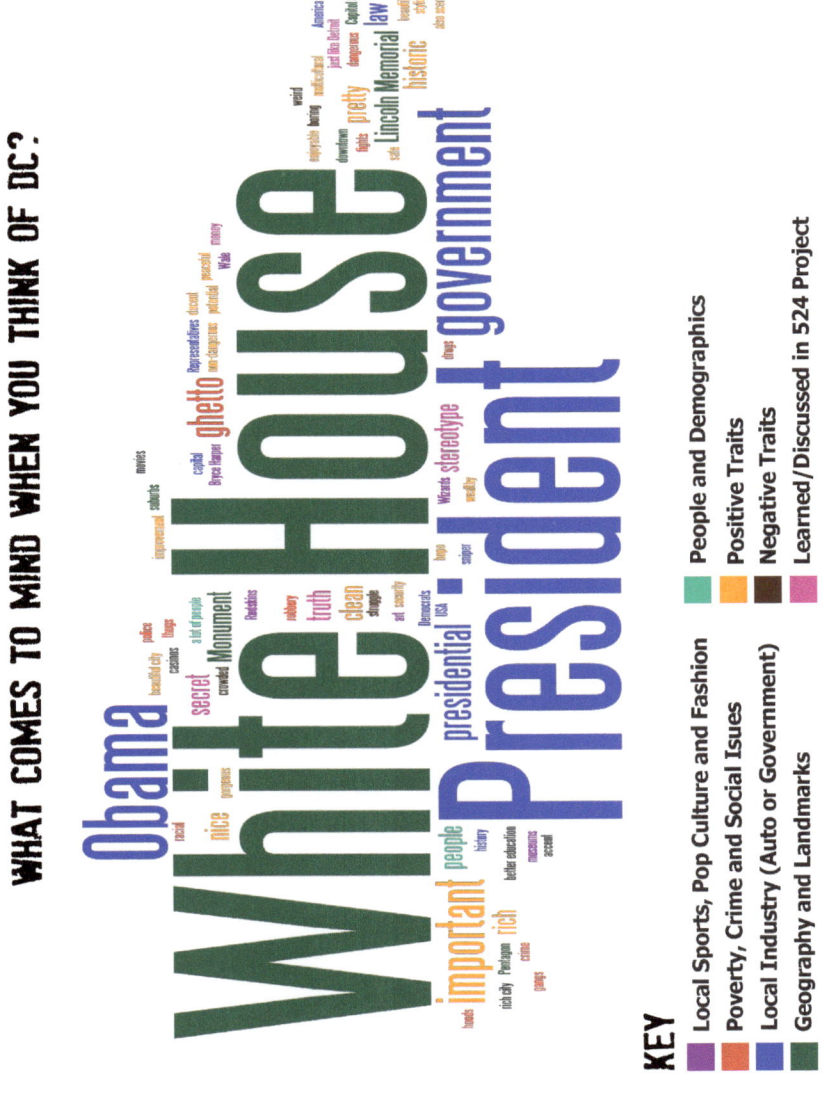

KEY

- **People and Demographics**
- **Positive Traits**
- **Negative Traits**
- **Learned/Discussed in 524 Project**
- **Local Sports, Pop Culture and Fashion**
- **Poverty, Crime and Social Issues**
- **Local Industry (Auto or Government)**
- **Geography and Landmarks**

DETROIT VIGNETTE 1:
I AM

I AM DETROIT
by *Leo Culver*

I am Detroit.
You think you know me.
You think that I am destructive and chaotic,
but actually, I am reconstructive and systematic.
I am the face and the mascot of my state.
I am the diamond in the rough– the up-and-coming underdog.
I am the small glare of light in the darkness.
I am the progress that comes with struggle,
   and I'll forever be hated for my appearance.
I am Detroit.

I AM DETROIT
by *Adrian Casillas*

I am Detroit.
You think you know me.
You think that I am
violent,
poor,
lazy,
uneducated.
But in reality
I am powerful,
overcoming obstacles that you throw my way.
My community is what makes me great.
I improve everyday.
You may not see what I am doing now or what I've done.
Later,
you will see what I have achieved.
What you said I couldn't do,
what I couldn't achieve,
but look at me now…
I am stronger than what you think I am. I will dominate
and eliminate the stereotypes.

I AM DETROIT
by *Diego Vasquez*

I am Detroit.
You think you know me.
You think that I am a rundown city and you want to put me out
    of my misery.
But really
I am in a whole new era.

DC VIGNETTE 2:
PERSPECTIVES IN CONFLICT

DC, YEARS FROM NOW
by *Will Richardson*

Five years from now, I see Southeast Washington, DC as what outsiders actually see it as. That being big buildings, new homes and great school systems. People in DC may change as well. I think that with all the new school buildings and homes, that wealthier people will move in and buy property.

I AM DC
by *Shawnquinette Davis*

I am DC.
You think you know me.
You think I'm a city with depression & cruel crimes
But really...
I am a city with lots of opportunity.

I'm born in the shape of a diamond.
Something so beautiful it's rarely seen
By the human's eye.

Depressed is what I'm not.
Full of soul is what I am.

TAKING THE TREE OUT OF THE GLITZ OF DC
by *Da'Nae Giles*

Characters:
DC
TREE

SCENE 1:

DC: I am DC. You think you know me.
You think I'm full of historical sites, museums and monuments.
You think because we have Obama here, we have it all.
But really I am full of poverty, full of crimes, murders, and
homicides. Full of graffiti and pissy train stations. Full of teens
who's not sure about what they want in life. You've only seen
the glitz & glams, but haven't seen the slums & rags.

TREE: I am a tree,
whose roots are planted down on the National Mall. I see
all types of people every day from across the world. From
Thomas Jefferson to the MLK Memorial, everything around
me is beautiful and green.

DC: You haven't seen all of me to judge me, or say how
beautiful I am.

TREE: I don't need to see all of you. I'm pretty sure everything's
the same.

DC: I'm going to take you and put you on the South side.

SCENE 2: One week later.

TREE: I've seen more than one part of the District...
everything isn't what it seems.
I saw the ghetto and the graffiti, which is still beautiful.
Now I know more than one DC.

DC AND THE MEDIA

by *Isaiah Prophet*

Characters:
MEDIA
DC

SCENE 1:

MEDIA: I hear 'bout homes a lot
but I feel like DC is like jazz,
it's cool to listen to but eventually
you want to hear more.
So I add words & a better beat
because people like to hear you doing good
but they're more interested when you're doing bad.
I just keep people interested
because the monuments and allat make y'all look sweet 'n all,
it's like y'all a beautiful city.
I'm just the pimples & unibrow hairs.
I just encourage the bad news to be heard more.

SCENE 2: MEDIA meets DC

MEDIA: You dressed very well.

DC: Thanks, it comes natural.

MEDIA: How you feeling?

DC: I'm always feeling good, very blessed.

MEDIA: Really?! With all that's going on in your life?

DC: (Looks at MEDIA) Watchu talm 'bout??

MEDIA: Seem like nothing's ever going right with you, it's always violence with you, I'm always hearing about the consistent deaths. I hear that even the air you breathe not sober.

DC: No... no no no, no not at all, you have everything confused.
All you're stating is the bad. You didn't mention all the good that overpowers it.
I am DC. You think you know me.
You think I'm between ghetto & glorious.
Most think I'm a cage with few openings.
Some view me as a great person just with big shadows.
Once you meet me and stop listening to rumors, you will find that though I have my flaws, my personality overpowers it.
I am actually a city of soul, that cage that you saw is actually a home full of opportunities & greatness.
Everything that makes me is made of pride.
You at a distance seeing garbage but once you get closer you'll see that we're treasure.
Put on shades because my talent may blind you.
Our bad side is our best side.

DETROIT VIGNETTE 2:
MY ART IS SO LOUD

MY ART IS SO LOUD
by *Josua Salazar*

My art is so loud it looks like nature taking back its land.
Abandoned buildings blooming with wildflowers and weeds.
The colorful sensations of graffiti adorning buildings and liquor stores.
The light show that the ambassador bridge engulfs the night sky.
The forces of people who have been hardened by downfalls
    and struggles.

My art is so loud it looks like a blast of colors
from the soft colors of my blue walls,
to the vibrant colors outside.
From seeing the bright yellow buses to the dull brown school building.
From seeing familiar faces to new faces.
From small, young joyful kids running around to the old couple
    hugging on their porch, all the way to the dog running around the
    park and the fresh green grass growing outside.
Just to end back in my own blue walls that I call my comfort zone.

My art is so loud it looks like it's coming to life.
Truth is it already had.
But so many of us lack the abilities to see it.
This is why Detroit shines. We see art everywhere.
We are the leaders of this state, of this country.
We have the first paved roads, the first mall.
We are, and always will be history.
We are leading this country in so many ways I could never be sure we
    are all the artists.
This city is our canvas…
All the buildings, sculptures, graffiti,
those are our paint strokes.

MY ART IS SO LOUD
by *Dorian Bryant*

My art is so loud
it looks like the Detroit Pistons back in '04.
My art looks like Michael Jordan soaring through the air.
Jumpman.
My art is so loud it looks like
Detroit,
DC,
together in harmony
creating greatness.

MY ART IS SO LOUD
by *Felix Lee*

My art is so loud
it looks like a shiny sun at noon.
My art is so ocean,
deep.
Unlimited like the numbers,
burning as the sun,
clean and white
snow before it falls down and touches the ground.
So tall
like the mountain Everest, and
hot like when a volcano spits out it's lava.

MY ART IS SO LOUD
by *Jessica Arias*

My art is so loud it looks like a bird soaring the sky
inspiring people
into wishing they could fly
alongside the bluejays
ravens
and other birds
in the endless blue sky.

DC VIGNETTE 3:
...AND SO IS MINE
(MY ART IS SO LOUD, PT.2)

MY ART IS SO LOUD
by *Callie Bizzell, Emoni Lowery, Sharhonda Lewis, Tanisha Phillips and Tiana Minter-El*

My art is so loud...
   It has to catch your attention.
   It feels like alcohol being poured into a wound.
   It feels like an old witch is scratching her nails on a blackboard.
   It feels like an earthquake cracking the ground.
   It feels like a loc being pulled out by its root.
   It feels like musical bass without decibel restrictions.
   It feels like drops of water creating an oceanic wave.

My art is so loud...
   It feels like the sweat of Curtis Mayfield baptizing me in soul while
   he sings "Superfly."

MY ART IS SO LOUD

by *Brittany Spencer, Da'Nae Giles, Iesha Crawford, Nadiya Holley and Will Richardson*

My art is so loud, it looks like me making something out of myself.
My art is so loud, it look like nothing or no art.
My art is so loud, it looks like a stadium screaming "M-V-P."
My art is so loud, it look like nothing or no art.
My art is so loud, it looks like uniforms dancing.
My art is so loud, it look like nothing or no art.

MY ART IS SO LOUD

by *Akim DeVille, Antonio Anderson, Damarco Morgan, Isaiah Prophet and Shawn Lee*

My art is so loud, it sounds like...
    Your mother giving you permission to go outside.
It sounds like...
    The cash register going ka-ching!
It sounds like...
    The crowd going wild after your performance.
It sounds like...
    A war chant from 300.
It sounds like...
    Your name being called at graduation.
It sounds like...
    You getting an acceptance letter to your top college.
It sounds like...
    That song you can't get out your head.
It sounds like...
    The crowd after you make the winning shot from half-court.
It sounds like...
    A timbale solo.
It sounds like...
    Yo' hood getting stamped at a go-go.
It sounds like...
    Your crush calling you bae.

DETROIT VIGNETTE 3:
SCENES OF THE CITY

WELCOME TO DETROIT
by *José Lopez*

RANDOM CITIZEN: Hello. You don't know me, and you never will, but today I will show you wonderful world known as Detroit. Well first of all, on my block nothing amazing happens. It's a pretty normal life. People just walk around no one is getting killed on a daily basis. People just live an average life. The mailman comes, people mow their lawns, no one truly lives in fear. So before you think anything of us, remember Detroit is just an average city. So don't say, "You suck!" or "There's too much violence." Chances are, we kinda are the same.

SOCIETY AGAINST OUTCAST
by *Rosario Ramirez*

I've been told that it's OK to be different, that it's good to not be like everyone else. But once you're "different" you get judged. People tell you you're a freak just because you don't have the same interests as them. I'm tired of being ridiculed. I'm tired of being put down, and I'm tired of being told it's OK to be different knowing that in the end I'm gonna be shamed for it.

SOCIETY: It's Ok to be different, I promise you. Different is...is great. At least you're not like everyone else in this world. You dress different, have a different styles, like a different type of music, and that's just amazing ...But...then again people are making fun of you, so I change my mind about what I said about being different. As for your taste in music...it's horrible! Why?'Cause not a lot of people like it...It's too "different."

SCENES OF THE CITY

by *Anonymous*

SCENE 1: at school

VIOLET: *(To herself)* I am close to graduating. My friends already
have plans for after they graduate. I don't. I'm good at a
lot of things, but I'm not passionate about anything. Why?

TEACHER: Do you have any ideas or plans for when you graduate?

VIOLET: Yea. I'm thinking maybe a police officer or a pastry chef.
But I'm not sure.

TEACHER: Well you better hurry up and pick a career that you
want to do soon, because your time is running out.

SCENE 2: Violet's bedroom

VIOLET: *(In bed, about to sleep.)* But what if I'm not good enough?
What if I mess up? What if no one likes me? What if I
embarass myself. I don't want to mess up. I'm going
to mess up my future. I'm going to end up like a damn
homeless person.
(Raises blanket up to her nose, eyes start watering.)
I shouldn't even try . I don't even want to be a police
officer or a pastry chef. Why couldn't I have been born
to the Kardashian family or some other rich family?
I wouldn't even need to do anything. I can't even do
anything without messing up. I'm awful at math. The only
thing I'm good at it messing up.

SCENE 3: *the next day at school*

TEACHER: Have you been accepted anywhere yet, Violet.?

VIOLET: No.

TEACHER: Remember, Violet, whatever you do right now in the present will forever affect your future. The present will either make you successful or fail miserably.
Try to be accepted.

SCENE 4: *at home in bed about to go to sleep*

VIOLET: No one is going to accept me. I'm not smart enough. I'm not good at anything. I don't even have plans for the future. Why bother trying when you know you aren't good enough? Why should I even care about anything. Everything would be a lot better if times stood still.
(Buries herself under blanket and silently cries.)
I'll never be successful. Why can't I just be smarter and care about stuff? I don't even have a purpose. I don't even have goals or reasons to be here. The past is in the past, they say, but history often repeats itself. I probably already messed everything up.
(Silently cries herself to sleep.)

DC VIGNETTE 4:
LOVE AND OTHER WORDS

LOVE

by *Sharhonda Lewis*
Final Presentation performance by *Precious Starks*

It's sweet, maybe sour,
It's painful, it's a power,
It's a smile, can be sung a song,
It's all right, can't be wrong.

It's a hug, it's a kiss,
It's humble, it's a bliss,
It's hard to do, it's easy,
It's complex, it's breezy.

It's caring, it's an emotion,
It leaves no one hopeless.

It's forgiving, it's appreciation,
It's passion, it's fashion,
It's anger, it's beauty,
It can be somewhat moody.

It consumes us all.
It comes down to the whole purpose of life –
It must be love.

LOVE LETTER TO DETROIT
by *Callie Bizzell*

Dear Detroit,

If you're gonna love me:
>   You need to know that I'm insecure and friendly.
>   You need to be respectful and be there for me when I'm down.
>   You need to do what you have to do to keep me happy and
>   motivated, to know that you're a true friend.

If you don't, I wouldn't be able to trust you or depend on you when you're needed.

But if you do, then I'll feel comfortable around you and be able to tell you about myself and personal life—to know you'll keep it a secret and not tell nobody...

Then I will love you back.

LOVE LETTER TO DETROIT
by *Akim DeVille*

Dear Detroit,

If you're gonna love me:
you need to know that I love you...
you need to be aware that DC is not all about violence...you need to do me a favor and know that this is not a game and if you do that, I will love you back.

LOVE LETTER TO DETROIT

by *Emoni Lowery*

Dear Detroit,

If you gonna love me you need to trust me.
You need to know I am from DC.
You need to be respectful toward me.
You need to do deeper research to know I am one of you.
I just live in a different city.

SOMETHING ABOUT DETROIT

by *Tanisha Phillips*

They saying that everybody think that Detroit is a bad city but they have positive things going on, like they have young people doing music and have them chasing they dreams. They have a lot of positive things going on downtown. They asking boys and girls to stick together and stop the killings because you don't want to be in jail, so you should stop, think and listen. They all in they 20's saying they trying to stop y'all people from being negative and tell them the things they did when they was that age, so they won't make the mistakes that they did. People go through things and it causes killings and a whole lot of stuff. They want Detroit to make a goal sheet and show people that they can reach them goals and finish school. Don't judge a book by its cover because Detroit is a good city.

LOVE LETTER TO DETROIT

by *Destini Simmons*

Dear Detroit,

You think you know us. We are not violent and disrespectful.
    You think we tried to diss but that wasn't our intent to.

You think you know the things of us as irrelevant.
    Is it because we share our city with the president?

We don't think less of you, more like get to know you.

Elaborate, there is more to us. No Golden Gate,
   more like us kids with A's straight
down the paper we chase.

I thought of you as just 8 Mile, a movie Eminem was in
    Rather than the fact of y'all good football team, Detroit Lions.

So don't think of us as just an
    ENEMY.

You are more to us, you are kin
    TO ME.

Don't think of this as an apology
    more like a prodigy.
524 Project is why we speak.
    Down the road and through the woods to Detroit,
where everything is the same as DC.

LOVE LETTER TO DETROIT

by *Nadiya Holley*

Dear Detroit,

If you're gonna love me
you need to know I am the STATES' CAPITAL.
I will have Fame.
Everyone knows who I AM.
You need to know
I am no different from you.
I am drama just like you.
I am the John Wall
while my residents are my fans.
I am so famous,
when I pull up on the
scene, red carpets
roll out and I
don't have to pay to
get into the club.
You need to be the
sun that brightens
my day and the
umbrella to block
the rain.
You need to do
what Texas or North Carolina won't do.
Just be Detroit. Do what you
expect from me.
What if you support me and accept my flaws...I will love
you back.

DETROIT VIGNETTE 4:
ROMANTIC POINT OF VIEW

LOVE ME
by *Daleecea McDaniel*

DC, if you're going to love me, trust
you should know that there's more to
me than appears.
Deeper.
Meaningful.
Maybe not to you, but to me.
You need to understand,
see past the beat up accents
instead of criticizing.
Think about it as a beautiful
tornado.
That's why they are named after women, right
see me as a woman
treat me right and see my wonders
do me wrong and see the mess I
make.
Love me.
Love my art.
Yes, graffiti is art.
My art.
As it tattoos on my body
enjoy my richness.
It's not in money, in culture
Diversity diferencia
No soy perfecta
Nor do I strive to be
Quiero amor
Necesito amor
But only if you let me be me
Por favor, aceptame

ROMANCE

by *Jackie Llamas*

MIND: Why do things always end up this way? We go round and round, but it never turns out the way we want. But I guess that's life, all the twists and turns you just got to go with it not having a choice or say what so ever. So now it's time to do what's best for me and move on.

HEART: I love him, I swear I do. I know he can change, he's not gonna cheat again. I know it, he wants to be with me. There's no way he doesn't. I mean, I give him everything. I always forgive him. He loves me. I know it.

MIND: You need to end it for good now.

HEART: No. He loves me. I love him.

MIND: There's no way it'll work. He's too selfish.

HEART: If I try hard enough if I change, it'll work.

MIND: No. He plays too many games. He doesn't love you. He doesn't...

HEART: Maybe it's me. Maybe I need to do things differently.

MIND: Or maybe you're blind. Maybe you're just gonna get broken again and again.

HEART: So maybe you're right. Maybe it's never gonna work. Maybe I need better, actually deserve better, and I'm gonna be strong enough to get it this time. This time, it's my choice.

ROMANCE

by *Jessica Chaven*

DC, if you're going to love me you must first know being scared is only temporary like the rain in Detroit. It comes and goes. So let fear leave and don't be afraid to love me, to know me. Because if you are going to love me you must know that I'm built up of beautiful things. I'm deep blue lakes, downtown skylines, and arenas of excitement. I am ballgames at Comerica Park and home runs ran to reach happiness. If you're going to love me you must know I am Detroit. The smiles of my people are the gateways to heaven. I'm the love of an unfailing mother, and the sound of my peoples greatness shakes the heaven and earth. If you're going to love me, DC I just hope you don't criticize but remember all the great things my city has done.

ROMANCE

by *Leo Culver*

DC, if you're going to love me, you must know I have experienced the struggle, but from the bottom up is the only way you can go. I am the all day hustler, but soon I will grow. With my grind I will shine through the rain and snow. I'll wait for my chance and on that day I will glow. DC, if you are going to love, you must be patient because soon enough I'll be too hot to touch, and on that day I want to look up and see that you were just waiting. Because that day we will be collaborating, and the whole world can only say congratulations. DC, this picture I'm painting isn't fabricated. DC, let's turn this picture into reality instead of imagining.

DC VIGNETTE 5: FREE YOUR VOICE... AND THE REST WILL FOLLOW

WHAT I SEE IN MY SCHOOL
by *Lamara Brooks*

What I see when I walk through my school: missing parts of the ceiling all on the floor, security guards walking around, red lights blinking on each door, kids walking around the hallway with pink, blue and yellow hair like a rainbow, words written on walls and desks, stamping their hoods. I hear the walkie-talkies and the metal detector going off as people walk through, I see the word BALLOU on the floor, people walking around asking, "Can I have my phone?" I see broke down lockers with trash hanging out. People running up and down the hallway screaming and banging on stuff. Walking through the hallway it smell so bad, all kinds of things mixed in one. I can hear the gates opening and closing, teachers so loud that you can hear them teaching in the hallway as you walk. Trash sitting in the water fountain as it run, lights flickering on and off because they broke, trash all on the floor, boy sitting in the windowsill just looking, people just sitting on the floor. What do you see in your school?

JUST A LIST OF THINGS: CARS, FOOTBALL AND THEM J'S

by *Shawnquinette Davis*

Young people flaunt their car, flexin' for ladies to get noticed, but them old folk around my way use them as a getaway, playing go-go music, dancing their hearts away.

On another note... Football is so stereotypical. You wanna be like RGIII, playing a sport, making millions, hoping to make a better life for family because you know the hood don't bring hopes & dreams, only fears & bad scenes.

J's for Jordans, fresh on a kid's feet. A new pair come out yesterday and on that same day a kid lost his life just for them J's.

I AM A PENNY

by *Iesha Crawford*

I am a penny.
I get spent all over DC,
Then I get dropped uptown.
People think less of my value,
So everyone walks past me, and across,
Like I don't matter.

5 YEARS AGO
by *Kyra Sheppard*

5 years ago, I was 11 years old.
Now, I'm 16 years old.
5 years from now, college is my future.

5 years ago, I graduated elementary.
Now, I'm in high school.
5 years from now, I'll be living large.

5 years ago, I won the drawing contest.
Now, I'm trying to survive high school.
5 years from now, I'll have 2 children.

5 years ago, I lost my Aunt Kim.
Now, I'm building a relationship with my mom.
5 years from now, I'll be working hard.

5 years ago, I used to get bullied.
Now, I get more respect as a young adult.
5 years from now, I'll watch lil sis
                              walk across the stage.

CRACK PIPE
by *Lamara Brooks*
Final Presentation performance by *Dwayne Whittaker*

Two crackheads fighting over me, trying to see who going to light
me up first. I'm almost older than both of them, but I've been with
her since she was 17—lighting me, I'm rusted and got a crack on my
head. I just look at her as she starts to talk to herself, eyes blood-shot
red. She looks at me, "You relieve my stress," but she runs me tired
round 10pm, that's when she really stresses. I'm tired and worn out.
I need a break and so does she—all she's doing is messing her life
up more. Ummm here she come with the lighter in her hand, time to
relieve her stress, looks like her boyfriend been beating on her again.
I'm not the only one with a crack on my head.

THE GO-GO DC SPOKEN WORD PIECE
by *Tiana Minter-El*

I want to articulate something to all you guys here
make sure you close your mouth and open your ears
because I got some important information y'all need to hear.

Uptown, Downtown, East of the River, and Capitol Hill
DC is the Frederick Douglass House coursing through my veins singing
sweet abolitionist blues
We Shall Overcome pulsates through the walls of the White House
because Americans had enough faith to let a Kenyan run this country
for the past 6 years.

The victors of struggle sit on the 92 with their gold medals cradled
in their arms, clinging to their shirts,
because their arms aren't long enough to grasp the rails.
Their wealth lies in their Safeway bags
because years of forced illiteracy allowed us to tap into the root
   of oral storytelling
so generations told generations how to create a novel of beautiful dishes
that their descendants should rob the nutrients from
and grow up and lay the mortar that my feet kisses as they worship
   the fact that
Stokely Carmichael shouted, "Hell no, we won't go" down these streets
because our king had been dethroned.

I am not telling you about DC
I am telling you what is DC
minus the adulteration, the rose-colored glasses of media portraying
   my city
yeah, I said it
my city
is only 2 miles of smiling
non-Washingtonians flashing their cameras at an area that
   Benjamin Banneker
gets no credit for.
DC is the crack pipes and AIDS rate equivalent to third world countries
but it's all good.
DC is the city that never forgot struggle but still stands on its feet
it is the place where you can make ketchup, hot sauce, sugar, and water
into a five star culinary creation.
DC is my home
and it is the best damn place to be.

DETROIT VIGNETTE 5
MY VOICE

ALL I SEE
by *Esmeralda Barco*

All I see in my neighborhood
is the beauty of the trees and snow.
I feel the wind blowing rapidly
against my cheeks.
I sense the smell of my neighbors
smoking a cigarette.
The touch of cold and freezing
snow every step I take.
Hearing the people walk
behind me talk about how was school.
Tasting the snowflakes when snow falls.
I would show the person how beautiful
my neighborhood is to me. Even though
there are smokers, it is a beautiful
place with profound memories.
I would show them a burnt
down house and the meaning
it meant to me. A family
could have had their whole life
in that house.
Also, tell them
what I saw that night while it burnt down.
Show them all the memories
of my neighborhood,
bad and good ones.

LIFE
by *Olivia Thumsey*

My mom is a book with a trillion pages.
Each chapter is a new personality.
Different characters every few pages.
Over a thousand different settings.
Never repeating a story, myth or legend.

My dad is a sword with no blade.
He swings and chops the air with
his imaginary weaponry.
He aims for a target that he'll never hit.

My sister is an ocean of Red Faygo.
She's fizzy and poppy.
She's syrupy joy.
She's happiness in a bottle
that makes you bloated the next day.

MY NEIGHBORHOOD
by *Jose Hernandez*

I live on a street where
you see little kids playing
on the sidewalk with chalk,
where you smell fresh bread
being produced by Brown's Buns Bakery.
Where you hear the echoes of the children laughing,
the swooshing of the air
through the rattling leaves of the the tall trees.
You would hear and see all the cars
that pass through Vernor, honking their horns.
You would taste the delicious cold ice cream
from the ice cream store on the corner.
You see all my friends outside
having fun, laughing together.
What I will always remember
about my neighborhood is the way
all my neighborhood treated me
when I moved in my house.

THE 524 PROJECT ASSESSMENT RESULTS

To measure the impact of **The 524 Project**, our students in Detroit and DC filled out self-assessment forms at the beginning and end of the program. These forms included questions about the students' experience of the program, their perceptions of both cities and their most lasting memories of **The 524 Project**. What follows is a representative sample of student responses from both DC and Detroit, as well as notable quotes from their post-program self-assessments.

BALLOU SENIOR HIGH SCHOOL SELF-ASSESSMENTS

- ■ Strongly Agree
- ■ Agree
- ■ Disagree
- ■ Strongly Disagree

Statement: "I am a good writer."

Pre-Assessment

Post-Assessment

Statement: "I know a lot about Detroit."

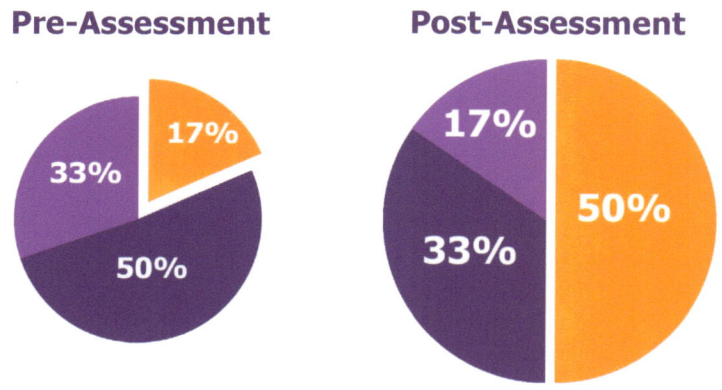

Pre-Assessment

Post-Assessment

> 66 Participating in **The 524 Project** made me think that my poetry could change my mind ... and **sharing it with others could open new doors for me.** 99

Rosario, **The 524 Project** Student

100% of participating Ballou High School students Agreed or Strongly Agreed to the statement "I am a good writer" by the end of the program. The number of participating students who Agreed to the statement "I know a lot about Detroit" **nearly tripled** over the course of **The 524 Project.**

WESTERN INTERNATIONAL HS SELF-ASSESSMENTS

- ■ Strongly Agree
- ■ Agree
- ■ Disagree
- ■ Strongly Disagree

Statement: "Others find my ideas interesting."

Pre-Assessment

9%
18%
45%
27%

Post-Assessment

27%
18%
55%

Statement: "I am proud of the city I live in."

Pre-Assessment

9%
27%
27%
36%

Post-Assessment

9%
18%
55%
27%

My Art Is So Loud

> **"** I hope that when the kids [in] **Washington, DC** see our films, they see what kind of amazing, great kids live here in **Detroit**. **"**

Diego, **The 524 Project** Student

73% of participating Western High School students Agreed or Strongly Agreed to the statement "Others find my ideas interesting" by the end of the program. The number of participating students who Strongly Agreed to the statement "I am proud of the city I live in" **doubled** over the course of **The 524 Project**.

THE ORGANIZATIONS

INSIDEOUT LITERARY ARTS PROJECT

By immersing students in the joy and power of poetry and literary self-expression, InsideOut Literary Arts Project inspires them to think broadly, create bravely and share their voices with the wider world. Guided by professional writers and celebrated by publications and performances, youth learn that their stories and ideas matter and that their pens can launch them off the page into extraordinary lives.

Experiencing the passion and transforming power of the written word will become an essential part of every child's education.

YOUNG PLAYWRIGHTS' THEATER

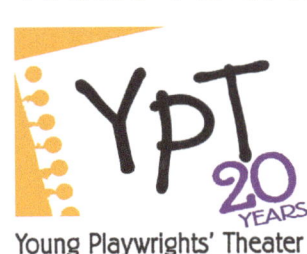

Young Playwrights' Theater inspires young people to realize the power of their own voices.

By teaching students to express themselves through the art of playwriting, YPT develops students' language skills, and empowers them with the creativity, confidence and critical thinking skills they need to succeed in school and beyond. YPT honors its students by involving them in a high-quality artistic process where they feel simultaneously respected and challenged and by engaging professional theater artists in producing student plays for the community.

www.ingramcontent.com/pod-product-compliance
Lightning Source LLC
Chambersburg PA
CBHW040744250626
47164CB00006BA/165